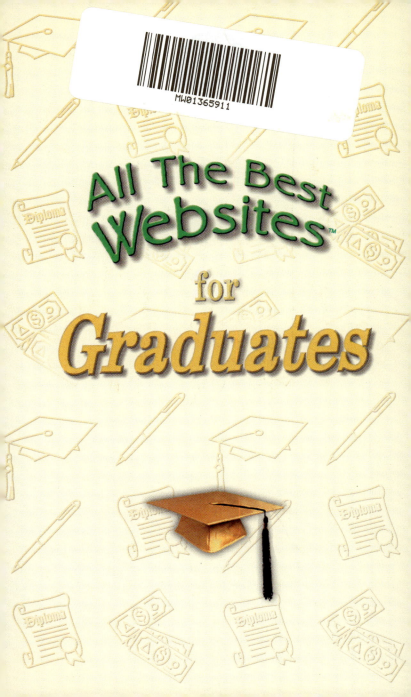

*All The Best Websites™ is not sponsored or endorsed by, or otherwise affiliated with, any of the websites or organizations referenced within. Any opinions expressed are solely those of the authors, and do not necessarily reflect those of the websites mentioned within.*

**All The Best Websites™ and the CheckerBee Web Guide™ are trademarks of CheckerBee, Inc.**

CheckerBee, Inc.
306 Industrial Park Road
Middletown, CT 06457
www.checkerbee.com

Copyright© 2001 CheckerBee, Inc.

All rights reserved. No part of this publication may be reproduced or transmitted in any form or by any means, electronic or mechanical, including photocopying, recording, or by any information storage or retrieval system, without the written permission of the publisher.

ISBN 1-58598-177-X

# Table Of Contents

**5  Introducing *All The Best Websites For Grads*™**

   **6** General Interest Sites

   **9** Continuing Your Education

 **14** Careers

 **23** Finding A Place To Live

 **30** Learning To Live On Your Own

 **37** Money, Finance & Investing

 **42** Diet, Health & Fitness

 **49** Love & Relationships

 **56** Going Out On The Town

**62** Movies, Music & More . . .

**68** Travel

**72** Style, Fashion & Beauty

**78** Shopping Sites

**83** Sites To Help You Simplify Your Life

**87** More Of The Best Websites

**94 Your Favorite Websites**

**95 E-mail Addresses**

# Introducing *All The Best Websites For Grads*™

Whether you've just graduated from high school, college or trade school, you stand in a unique period of transition, moving out of one life and into the next. This is an exciting time; the world is out there waiting for you! A thousand choices are now yours: whether to continue in school or enter a career; where you'll live (and with whom); what you'll do with all the time you used to spend studying; even how you'll dress, now that you're headed for the big time!

As transitions can also be scary, it helps to collect as many resources as possible. The more you know about your options, the better prepared you'll be to choose one (or two, or ten!) of them. In this day and age, the Internet is among the top tools for people, like yourself, who want a lot of information, on a lot of subjects, in an easily-accessible form.

This book is an Internet directory designed with recent graduates in mind. In it, you will find some of the best websites to consult on serious subjects like finding a job or managing your money, as well as on fun topics, such as nightlife, shopping and travel. We've even thrown in a few sites that everyone needs sooner or later, like those which can give you directions, help you write a businessletter, or find those old classmates you've lost touch with. So fire up your computer, Graduate; it's time to start surfing!

Introducing *All The Best Websites For Grads*™   5

# General Interest Websites

While there are a lot of websites out there that contain material on very specific subjects, some are remarkable because they cover just about everything, with dozens of topics, links to zillions more sites and everything from news, to search engines, to message boards and chat rooms. People who know they'll be looking for something different every time they log on often use one of these sites as their home page (the one that comes up on the screen automatically), so they'll have quick access to whatever's on their minds. Another alternative is to bookmark your favorites, so when you need them, they're within clicking distance.

This chapter is devoted to just such general-interest web pages, both those with search engines and those without, as well as some which collect links to help you narrow down your search. You don't necessarily even have to know what you want when you use these sites. Say one day you're sitting around thinking, "I'm bored." You log onto a general-purpose website and see categories for entertainment, education, travel, and lifestyle – and suddenly you start asking yourself, "What kind of bored?" You can download a computer game or check out a cyber-soap opera. Are you in the mood for entertainment? You can look up movie showtimes in your area or find out about local museum exhibits and ball games. Bored with your whole life? Dig into the education category or surf bargain travel websites for ideas on places where you can go to get away from it all. Ready? Let's go!

# about.com

*Calling itself "The Human Internet," about.com has thousands of experts on just about any subject you can think of.*

▶ Tips, columns and chats on everything from agnosticism to rodeos.

▶ News center features the day's headlines, weather and "weird news."

▶ E-mail newsletter will send highlights to your inbox.

# excite.com

*One of the most popular multi-purpose websites, you can personalize excite.com to show the topics you want to see.*

▶ Free e-mail available and an easy-to-use search engine.

▶ Personal tools include address books and calendars.

▶ Lots of downloads – wallpaper, MP3s, and more.

# msn.com

*Check your e-mail, the daily news (courtesy of MSNBC) and explore a comprehensive list of "Internet channels" on the ever popular msn.com.*

▶ Free e-mail, planners, news and stock quotes.

▶ Meet people and chat with friends.

▶ Download games, send greeting cards and shop for virtually anything.

▶ Create your own web community.

General Interest Websites

## General Interest Websites

Are you looking for an informative homepage? Or maybe you need space to store a site of your own creation. Check out these sites to find the perfect fit for you.

---

**100hot**.com – *the best sites on the 'net divided by category*

**ask**.com – *Jeeves is ready to find answers to all your questions*

**delphi**.com – *various interactive forums and a web search*

**dogpile**.com – *a great engine and not as messy as it sounds*

**earthlink**.net – *this IP's homepage offers hosting and surfing*

**efront**.com – *a web directory, plus entertainment resources*

**go**.com – *news from ABC, ESPN and Disney*

**gohip**.com – *serves all your needs, from finances to MP3s*

**google**.com – *easy-to-use search engine and directory*

**iwon**.com – *as you search the web, you could win lots of cash*

**lcweb.loc**.gov – *research anything at The Library of Congress*

**looksmart**.com – *a comprehensive web directory*

**mamma**.com – *"The mother of all search engines"*

**metacrawler**.com – *a search engine you can customize*

**profusion**.com – *a powerful multi-website search engine*

**refdesk**.com – *almanac, homework helper and news from AP*

**search**.com – *search either their site or the entire Internet*

**snowball**.com – *Internet search, e-mail and message boards*

**terra**.com – *this site is available in both English and Spanish*

**time**.com – *TIME magazine's home, for current affairs junkies*

**top50**.com – *a categorized list of the 50 best 'net sites*

**webcrawler**.com – *search, pick up headlines and chat here*

**yahoo**.com – *a classic web search and e-mail provider*

# Continuing Your Education

Yes, you've graduated, but that doesn't mean your learning life is over. The healthiest minds never stop growing and taking in new ideas. Some people stay mentally active by continuing with college or graduate school, while others join discussion or reading groups, enroll in non-credit personal development courses, or regularly attend seminars related to their careers. As a recent graduate, your mind is still familiar with the learning process, so you're in a perfect position to continue nurturing it, expanding it, helping it thrive.

To aid you in this process, we've collected some of the best resources to help you feed your mind, whether you intend to go for more formal schooling, just want to take a class here or there, or need quick instructions on solving everyday problems like how to invest your hard-earned cash. In fact, we've even supplied websites to help you if you're already enrolled as a student.

Remember that part of healthy mental activity involves having fun with the learning process, so look for opportunities to learn what you like, and not only what you need. Browse sites thoroughly to see what they offer and be open to trying new things. In the process of  looking for computer seminars, you just might run across, say, a great class in learning the cheeses of Italy. So, if that's what appeals to you, go for it! Who says cheese-tasting isn't educational?

# **bartleby**.com

*Categorized by reference, verse, fiction and nonfiction, Bartleby is the forerunner of e-published classics.*

- Visit every day for new biographies, defined words, quotations and poetry.

- It's also the home of *Bartlett's Familiar Quotations*.

- Purchase books and e-books at the Bartleby bookstore.

# **britannica**.com

*Yes, the classic encyclopedia is accessible on-line and even features news articles.*

- Search the database to find information instantly.

- You can join in on the "Britannica Forums" to voice your opinions and expertise.

- Let Britannica help you find other educational resources, including scholarship money.

# **collegeboard**.org

*The College Board has helped students get into colleges and adjust to student life for a century.*

- Register and prepare for your standardized tests.

- Find a college that suits you.

- Use their guide to how to apply to schools to stay informed and find answers to your pressing questions.

# finaid.com

*Not going anywhere without financial aid? This guide to loans, grants and scholarships will help you decide which programs are best for you and your financial future.*

- Find out which scholarships you're eligible for and use the calculator tools to figure out how much money you need.
- Download financial aid forms with instructions for filling them out correctly.
- "Ask the Advisor" provides answers to your questions.

# kaplan.com

*Kaplan offers resources for standardized test and licensing preparation as well as continuing education.*

- Order books and software to study for every exam from the SAT to the NCLEX, or browse on-line.
- "Kaplan College" offers a variety of on-line degrees.
- Receive training for professional certifications from real estate to insurance.

# learn2.com

*For less formal, practical learning, turn to learn2.com.*

- Among the no-cost tutorials are "Learn2 Cope With Insomnia" and "Learn2 Fix a Bike Flat."
- "Learnlines Forum" discussion groups let learners share tips.

## oed.com

*The on-line home of the Oxford English Dictionary is the premier site for all your definition and usage needs.*

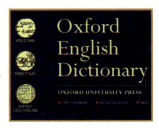

- The OED defines words and lists their etymologic history, spelling variations and pronunciation.
- Includes full-sentence quotations to further explain proper usage.
- Visit regularly to check out the "word of the day."

## petersons.com

*An invaluable resource on colleges, graduate programs, financial aid and everything else study-related.*

- Distance learning programs (on-line courses, correspondence courses, etc.) are now listed.
- Information on test preparation is available.
- Extensive school listings include details such as size of student body, majors available, tuition costs and more.

## studyabroad.com

*Interested in studying overseas? This website lets you find study abroad programs by subject, by country and by language. Includes travel info, maps and much more!*

- Contains links to schools with international study programs.
- "Adventure Travel Finder" helps locate learning vacations.
- Scholarship and financial aid info.

# Websites On Education

Check out these sites to help you research term papers, apply for financial aid, continue your education or just find a good dictionary.

---

**allaboutcollege**.com – *a great starting point for basic info*

**amillionlives**.com – *links to biographical info on the Web*

**bbc**.co.uk/education/home – *history and science for all ages*

**bibliomania**.com – *reference and study guides, plus classic lit*

**bigchalk**.com – *geared at kids but offers great basic info*

**classics.mit**.edu – *e-texts from the "Internet Classics Archive"*

**encarta.msn**.com – *college searches and an encyclopedia*

**estudentloan**.com – *use the loan finder to compare rates*

**factfinder.census**.gov – *find stats about the United States*

**ilearn**.com – *comprehensive portal site for distance learning*

**ipl**.org – *reference, on-line magazines and literature texts*

**itools**.com – *language, reference and research tools*

**m-w**.com – *Merriam-Webster Dictionary and Thesaurus*

**nypl**.org – *research libraries, catalogs and e-resources*

**parlo**.com – *free foreign language lessons via e-mail*

**princetonreview**.com – *take on-line test prep classes*

**promo**.net/pg – *download Project Gutenberg's e-texts*

**recruiter.embark**.com – *sign up and let schools find you*

**review**.com – *law, medical, grad and undergrad resources*

**salliemae**.com – *includes a glossary of financial aid terms*

**sparknotes**.com – *study guides from literature to nutrition*

**studentadvantage**.com – *discounts and campus life info*

**utexas**.edu/world/lecture – *links to on-line courses*

# Careers

Like many American students, you may have had jobs while you were in school, but the working world seems like a different place when your job, rather than your coursework, is the focus of your day. No longer just a means of earning pocket money, satisfying employment is now the source of your independence – a way to keep yourself housed, fed, clothed, and entertained in ways that make you happy.

However, not everyone has the same definition of a "good" job; for some, the idea is to make as much money as possible, while others are looking for work which is exciting or fun. Therefore, it's as important to know what you're looking for in a job as it is to know what kind of job you're qualified for; you're more likely to find a fulfilling career if you're clear, from the outset, on your criteria.

The first step, of course, is to find out what positions are available and, to that end, this chapter gives you resources for browsing employment listings. As was true with the education sites, try to be open to new ideas or you might miss a super position just because it wasn't listed specifically under one category. If, instead of looking for a new job, you're interested in staying competitive in your current one, check out the resources we've found which cater to career-minded people; both those looking for training and those trying to stay current in their profession.

# aboutjobs.com

*Where else can you look for a job everywhere from a ski resort to an accounting firm? Aboutjobs.com and its four sub-sites are tailored to your specific employment needs.*

- Search for summer jobs and internships, as well as corporate positions.
- Sign up for their mailing list to get site updates.
- Look for jobs overseas.

# assessment.com

*Not quite sure which industry is right for you? The Motivational Appraisal of Personal Potential (MAPP) site can help you find the right career path.*

- Free career analysis.
- Personalized job search provided at discounted rates.
- Student and personal appraisals are also offered.

# black-collegian.com

*The ultimate source for African-American and other minority students, this site celebrates diversity. Learn about grad school, military and corporate opportunities.*

- Read about African-American history and social issues.
- Search the military and corporate job bank.
- Post your résumé.

# careerbuilder.com

*You can search jobs from over 75 Internet sites and read pertinent news stories and updates about current trends in the working environment.*

▶ Get résumé advice, career counseling and interview tips.

▶ The site is equipped with a "Salary Wizard."

▶ Visit the "Tech Lounge."

# careermag.com

*A tool for both job seekers and the gainfully employed, careermag.com covers job issues such as affirmative action, management skills and sales strategies.*

▶ Weekly survey for a chance to win $100.

▶ E-mail newsletter.

▶ On-line courses (offered for a fee) cover career building, workplace safety and information technology.

# careerplanit.com

*CareerPlanit's "galaxy of career possibilities" has information and interactive tools to help you get the perfect job.*

▶ Check out employer profiles to see who's doing the hiring.

▶ Interact with others in the site's "Communication Station."

▶ Search for both internships and full-time jobs.

16  Careers

# collegegrad.com

*The "#1 Entry Level Job Site" will help you write a résumé, as well as teach you interview and salary-negotiation skills.*

- Search for entry-level and internship jobs.
- Listen to tutorials and read the *Job Hunter E-Zine*.
- Question and answer forum with author, Brian Krueger.

# councilexchanges.org

*Do you want to work overseas? Employers and future employees from all around the world meet at this Internet hotspot.*

- Resources for teachers looking for overseas classrooms.
- Host a student from a foreign country.
- Search career opportunities or look to further your education abroad.

# dice.com

*The information technology field is growing. Hit dice.com to find out about job opportunities near you.*

- Search jobs by region.
- Store résumés on-line and get e-mailed job postings.
- Prepare for your upcoming certification exams.

Careers 17

## dol.gov

*Everyone should visit the homepage for the Department of Labor. Find out what your rights are in the workplace.*

- Link to America's Job Bank.
- In-depth articles on how to maximize your benefits.
- Are you part of the norm? Research national employment statistics.

## govtjobs.com

*If you're interested in working in the public sector, visit govtjobs.com for government job resources and opportunities.*

- Highly detailed postings.
- Job listings are for government offices and non-profit companies.
- Links to state government websites.

## hoovers.com

*It's not a site about vacuum cleaners (though, your room probably needs one). Hoover's Online is a network for businesses and their employees.*

- Hundreds of company and industry profiles.
- Sign up for newsletters.
- Info on career development and business travel.
- Links to other sites.

# hotjobs.com

*One of the first job search sites, hotjobs.com allows you to search for employment by company, industry and location.*

- Career channels let you browse through jobs.
- Visit the "HotJobs Career Expo" or voice your opinion at one of the "HotJobs Forums."
- Post your résumé and let employers find you.
- Personalize your own "myHotJobs" page.

# job-interview.net

*With thousands of interview questions and links to interviewing tips, this site is like a seminar in how to woo a recruiter!*

- Practice interviews and answer strategies.
- Practical advice, such as how long to wait after an interview before calling back.
- Job specific tips.

# jobsonline.com

*An endless source of information, jobsonline.com proves that "Knowledge is Power."*

- On-line training and job search tutorials.
- Information on relocating.
- Research the best companies and find local career fairs.

Careers 19

# mediabistro.com

*A comprehensive and witty "e-zine" for media professionals, mediabistro.com provides job searches, as well as industry news and updates.*

- Feature articles and a "question of the week" forum.
- Post your résumé.
- On-line help with their "Résumé Builder."

# monster.com

*Widely-used by hiring companies and job seekers alike, monster.com lets you post your résumé on-line where recruiters can find it.*

- Huge database of jobs in the United States and abroad.
- Résumé-building center offers tutorials on writing the perfect résumé and includes sample résumés and cover letters with "Do's and Don'ts."
- Take a "virtual" job interview, then rate how you did.

The monsters at *monster.com* can show you the way to a new career.

# peacecorps.gov

*Looking for a bigger, better adventure? Why not join the Peace Corps?*

- Find recruiting events near you.
- Stories from volunteers and worldwide news.
- Apply for the Peace Corps on-line.

# quintcareers.com

*Subtitled the "career and job hunting resources guide," quintcareers.com is a goldmine for job seekers, with links to terrific job sites and professional services.*

- Résumé distribution, career articles and tutorials.
- Advice and tips for those attending college.
- Links to cool, unusual and seasonal jobs.

# seminarinformation.com

*More than 360,000 career-related seminars (live and in-person) are listed here, along with their dates, locations, and costs.*

- Search engine helps you find what you're looking for fast.
- On-line enrollment.
- Lists trade shows, career and personal development seminars and costs.

# vault.com

*Dubbed "the insider career network," vault.com can help you find a new job or cope with the one you have.*

- Contains message boards, a multimedia center and a résumé database.
- Breaking news on a multitude of industries.
- They'll e-mail you suitable job postings.

## More Great Career Sites

Whether you're in the job market or you just want to survive life behind a desk, these sites are for you.

**americanjobs**.com – *high-tech and engineering jobs*

**careerfitter**.com – *take a test to see where you belong*

**communityjobs**.org – *search for non-profit jobs*

**ejobs**.org – *find environmental jobs and internships*

**flipdog**.com – *a job search site with a sense of humor*

**headhunter**.net – *job info that comes with a "panic button"*

**higheredjobs**.com – *find jobs at colleges and universities*

**jobdirect**.com – *search the database or create a profile*

**jobs**.com – *résumé writing, communities and career fairs*

**jobsingovernment**.com – *search for jobs in government*

**jobsleuth**.com – *daily news headlines, stories and trivia*

**jobtrak**.com – *on-line career fairs and networking*

**jobweb**.com – *job search and tips on life after college*

**lawjobs**.com – *center for job information and industry news*

**marketingjobs**.com – *search for marketing jobs nationwide*

**net-temps**.com – *jobs for those not quite ready for full-time*

**newsjobs**.com – *diversity-related journalism opportunities*

**pnnonline**.org – *searches and info on non-profit companies*

**salary**.com – *find out how much you should be making*

**sciencejobs**.com – *for careers in bioscience and chemistry*

**sunoasis**.com – *writers and editors need look no further*

**tvjobs**.com – *search for jobs in the broadcast industry*

**wetfeet**.com - *helping you stay informed about your career*

**writerswrite**.com – *a hotspot for writers and publishers*

# Finding A Place To Live

Nothing is more exciting than settling into a new living space, one you chose yourself and can arrange, decorate, and furnish any way you like. The possibilities are limitless. How you live and with what you surround yourself define you as a person and when you start with four bare walls and a floor, that definition is totally and entirely up to you. Whether you choose a style that's utilitarian, traditional or shabby-chic, your surroundings will reflect your own self-image.

First, you've got to find that new, personality-defining, living space! If you've never lived on your own, you will probably need advice on where to look and what's involved in a household move. Some of the websites in this chapter aim to help you find the perfect city or neighborhood, while others are designed to locate a specific property in that area.

A large apartment complex isn't the only place to find housing (although, if that's your style, you might just find one with a pool!); you can look for a townhouse, a multi-family home (like a duplex or even a four-plex), or perhaps something like a "mother-in-law" apartment in a private home. If you're on a tight budget, you can search for a single room in a shared house or use roommate-finder listings. Then, when you've found your new digs, look into the sites that specialize in moving services.

Finding A Place To Live 23

## apartments.com

*Choose the state you want from a map, then pick your town and enter criteria like price range and the search engine will bring up listings from local classified ads and other websites.*

- ▸ Take virtual apartment tours.
- ▸ Includes links to roommate referral services, moving companies and companies that offer renter's insurance.
- ▸ Allows you to refine your search by including housing amenities – pool, dishwasher, etc.

## citysearch.com

*With links to websites for major cities both here and abroad, citysearch.com can help you "interview" your new town before you get there.*

- ▸ Has guides to nightlife and entertainment.
- ▸ Enter your zip code for even more specific information.
- ▸ Find news and events virtually anywhere in the world.

## collegeroommates.net

*Tired of stepping out of bed into a half-eaten pizza? Can't find your laundry because your roomie is wearing most of it? If you're thinking of swapping roommates, check out this site.*

- ▸ Read the roommate horror stories for a few good laughs.
- ▸ What to expect from roommates in a dorm or apartment.
- ▸ How to interview potential roommates.

Need a new roomie? *Collegeroommates.com* can help!

24   Finding A Place To Live

# digitalcity.com

*A world of fun is merely a zip code away. Be sure to check out digitalcity.com if you're looking to see what there is to do in a prospective new town.*

▶ Search by state, town name or zip code.

▶ Chat with the locals and get a visitor's guide for each city.

▶ Find out where to shop and where to go for the best live entertainment.

# monstermoving.com

*The job search site that you've grown to love is now helping you move, too.*

▶ Plan your move with their on-line calendar.

▶ Get information on a mortgage or insurance quotes.

▶ Notify the U.S. Post Office of your new mailing address.

This creature from *monstermoving.com* can help you find new digs.

# move.com

*Whether you're buying, selling or renting, move.com will eliminate the stress of your moving adventure.*

▶ Search for an apartment that has all of the amenities you're looking for.

▶ Check out schools, price rates and other pertinent neighborhood information.

▶ Set up utilities and services before you even move in.

Finding A Place To Live   25

## moving.com

*They offer the "complete relocation solution" for those in the process of moving or just wondering about where the best place to live is.*

▶ Use their financial services and real estate listings to plan your big move.

▶ Comparison shop between different moving companies and neighborhoods.

▶ Get information on the best ways to pack your stuff.

## movingcenter.com

*This all-purpose moving site has advice on truck rental, moving companies, packing supplies, self-storage and more.*

▶ Has a searchable apartment-finder.

▶ Site tools include a checklist and an expense calculator.

▶ Gives advice on phone, utility, and cable services.

## mycounsel.com

*In their "Landlord/Tenant" section, read about your rights as a tenant.*

▶ Regularly changing topics of discussion ranging from pet issues to eviction.

▶ Submit your questions to "Stanley," the resident lawyer.

▶ What to look for in a good (or bad) lease.

Finding A Place To Live

# nolo.com/chapter/evten/evten_law_ch7_a.html

*This sample chapter from Nolo's "Every Tenant's Legal Guide" gives practical advice on how to live with roommates and each person's rights and responsibilities.*

- Book is available for sale on the site.
- Gives examples of co-living situations, problems and outcomes.
- Suggests ground rules to establish before moving in with someone.

# places4rent.com

*Lists house and apartment rentals in the U.S. and Canada, as well as links to moving-related sites.*

- Offers good links to moving companies, roommate referral services and sub-lease situations.
- Place a wanted ad and let landlords respond to you!
- Approved by the Better Business Bureau On-line.

# rent.net

*Use rent.net's resources to answer all your moving questions, including finding apartments and corporate housing.*

- Learn about renting furniture – an easy way to save some extra cash.
- They'll connect and disconnect your utilities for you.
- Find a roommate.

Finding A Place To Live 27

# roommateclick.com

*This popular roommate-matching site allows you to search for a housing partner by age, sex and geographical area.*

- Includes potential roommates with rooms to rent, or who are looking for rooms.
- Some ads have photos.
- Ads include smoking preferences, sexual preferences and other important criteria.

# roommatefind.com

*Sign up for their free roommate matching service to find the perfect roommate in your area.*

- Read success stories on their testimonials page.
- Check out their resource center for helpful tips, a "Survival Guide" and moving tools.
- Take the "Roommate Compatibility Quiz" to see how you and potential roommates match up.

# uhaul.com

*For the do-it-yourself mover, this site provides you with trucks or trailers, trailer hitches for your car and all the supplies you'll need to help you with your move.*

- Buy boxes, furniture pads and storage space.
- On-line reservations and rate quotes.
- Frequent special deals.

Finding A Place To Live

# Sites That Will Move You

Moving can be a complex process, but with these Internet resources, you can get off to an informed start. Look here for everything from supplies to address correction.

---

**addresscorrection**.com – *tell everyone your new address*

**allboxes**.com – *order moving supplies and have them shipped*

**apartmentguide**.com – *find and furnish an apartment*

**apartmentsearch**.com – *search apartments nationwide*

**apartmentsnationwide**.com – *find an apartment or office*

**apartmentsusa**.com – *check out apartments and roomies*

**apartmentworld**.com – *see photos and tour apartments*

**apartmentzone**.com – *find apartments in Chicago*

**aptsforrent**.com – *the homepage of For Rent magazine*

**cities**.com – *find events and info for cities around the globe*

**heretoanywhere**.com – *search for temporary housing*

**homescape**.com – *rent, find roomies and get current news*

**imove**.com – *plan your move or hire a moving company*

**makethemove**.com – *relocation service and utility transfer*

**mlx**.com – *"Manhattan's Largest Database" of living spaces*

**mooving**.com – *moving supplies and packing tips*

**roomfind**.com – *check out the daily featured roommate*

**roomie**.com – *submit your profile and find a roommate*

**roomiematch**.com – *roommate seekers e-mail you directly*

**roommatelocator**.com – *find roommates in any country*

**roommatesonline**.com – *browse their roommate database*

**timeout**.com – *search worldwide with London's living guide*

**vanlines**.com – *check out movers and relocation companies*

# Learning To Live On Your Own

Okay, you've got the new apartment (with a diploma on the wall!), the satisfying job and the freedom to live life on your own terms. Terrific! At some point, though, it may hit you that you could still use a little help with some of the skills we all need to live in the real world.

On any given day, you might flood the bathroom, ruin the mini-blinds, or even have a dinner guest, and suddenly find that you need a little assistance with the details: dealing with water damage, installing new window treatments, or planning a menu beyond boxed mac and cheese. Fortunately, a wealth of information is available on these "life-skills" and all you have to do is find it.

To start you on your way, we offer helpful websites on cooking, decorating and home repair. It helps, obviously, to know some of these things before you need to use them, so why not browse the internet now? Don't assume that, just because your landlord is responsible for your building, you'll never need to know about setting a door hinge; sometimes it's easier to fix the cabinet door yourself than to wait until someone else gets around to doing it. There's an added bonus, as well: the more stuff you can do yourself, the more independent you'll feel!

## allabouthome.com

*Sponsored by ServiceMaster, this site gives advice on all aspects of owning or renting a home.*

▶ Money-saving coupons for everything from pest control to plumbing services.

▶ Sub-sections under "Cleaning Tips for your Home" give specific directions on how to deal with almost any stain.

## bhglive.com

*This virtual version of Better Homes and Gardens magazine gives tips on everything from how to plan a party to which plants will grow best in your garden.*

▶ How to plan everything from a casual get-together with friends to a sit-down dinner with the boss.

▶ Lots of recipes and craft ideas!

▶ A bulletin board where you can find advice on conquering your decorating dilemmas.

## digsmagazine.com

*Calling itself a "a home + living guide for the post-college, pre-parenthood, quasi-adult generation," this site is perfect for the first-time apartment dweller.*

▶ Gives ideas for hosting friends in your new place.

▶ Relaxation section suggests movies, drinks and more.

▶ Magazine comes out every Monday and Thursday.

Learning To Live On Your Own

## doityourself.com

*If you're moving out on your own for the first time, you don't want to miss this website!*

▶ Features hints, tips and tricks on building and landscaping to save you time and money.

▶ Community forums hosted by do-it-yourself experts.

▶ Information on mortgages and loans.

## epicurious.com

*An all-around wonderful site for gourmet cooking that's loaded with recipes, discussion groups, cookbook reviews and more.*

▶ Recipe browser searches archives of food magazines.

▶ Each issue features new drink and food recipes and menu ideas.

▶ E-mail newsletter will bring recipes to your inbox.

## fema.gov/pte/prep.htm

*Not to scare you, but in case you live in an area prone to natural disaster, you might want to visit this site.*

▶ Organized by type of disaster, the Federal Emergency Management Agency website tells you what to do in each situation.

▶ Advice also given on winter driving.

▶ Suggests how to remain safe during other dangerous situations like house fires and acts of terrorism.

Learning To Live On Your Own

## frugal-moms.com

*Even if you're not a mom, this magazine's subtitle – "Live Better for Less" – should make you sit up and take notice.*

▶ Filled with cheap ways to decorate, garden and keep yourself healthy.

▶ The site focuses on finding different methods of budget-conscious living.

▶ Several different newsletters, some sent out daily.

## fsis.usda.gov

*Since you are now in charge of the groceries, why not take a few hints from the USDA on food safety and what to look for on the labels?*

▶ The latest nutritional news and information.

▶ The answers to many frequently asked questions.

▶ How to obtain publications on food safety and handling.

## furniturewizard.com

*Here you'll learn to repair and refinish furniture and have it looking brand new in no time.*

▶ How to get those pesky water rings off tables.

▶ Step-by-step refinishing projects for beginners.

▶ Recommendations on books, videos and supplies.

▶ Tip-sharing discussion groups.

Learning To Live On Your Own

## **garden**.org

*Even those who have the blackest thumb will be able to get something out of this comprehensive and well-laid-out site.*

- Regional weather reports so you can monitor how your plants will fare.

- How-to projects, on-line courses and articles to help you with any gardening project.

- A gardening dictionary to help you translate scientific names into common ones.


## **goodkarmacafe**.com

*This is one of the best vegetarian cooking websites on the 'net, with everything from recipes and nutrition guides to book reviews.*

- A guide to vegetarian restaurants across the nation.

- Offers free veggie postcards with recipes on the back.

- A recipe exchange where you can swap favorites with other on-line visitors.


## **hammerzone**.com

*Updated often, this handyman's dream offers projects for do-it-yourselfers of every level.*

- Specializes in home repairs, remodeling and construction.

- Post your experiences so others can admire your handiwork.

- "Planet of Links" sends you to other great sites.

Learning To Live On Your Own

## marthastewart.com

*Whether you're looking for a crafty holiday display or to get your garage organized, Martha knows how to do it with efficiency and flair.*

- ▶ Features a guide to choosing the right lighting.
- ▶ A "tag sale" section directs you to special bargains.
- ▶ "Channels" on everything from weddings to babies.

## messygourmet.com

*"If you burn a dish - Call it 'well-done.' If you undercook a dish - Call it 'al dente,'" advises this website for the culinarily-challenged.*

- ▶ Filled with humorous (but helpful!) tips on making a mess and then cleaning it up!
- ▶ Features a guide to the some of the coolest gadgets that will make your time in the kitchen a lot less stressful.

- ▶ Advice from visitors on how to combat stains.

## organizedhome.com

*This website gives helpful advice on getting – and keeping – your place organized.*

- ▶ Offers printable planners, checklists, and forms for household organizing.
- ▶ Covers storage, cleaning, and time management.
- ▶ Suggestions on how to save money, too!

Learning To Live On Your Own

# Websites To Help You Help Yourself

Want more? Whether you are looking for a new project or need help with a current one, there is a site here for you.

**artoffengshuiinc**.com – *arrange your home for good health*
**cheftalk**.com – *learn how to cook from the pros*
**cooking**.com – *register for gifts or buy them for yourself*
**culinarycafe**.com – *the tools, tips and techniques you need*
**decorating-your-home**.com – *makeovers for every room*
**decoratingstudio**.com – *everything from fabrics to floors*
**foodandwine**.com – *features recipes and a wine guide*
**foodtv**.com – *all of the network's shows at your fingertips*
**gardenguides**.com – *catalogs, scrapbooks and plant guides*
**gardenweb**.com – *a calendar of events and supply trading*
**hgtv**.com – *Home & Garden Television on the web*
**homearts**.com – *tips and articles from popular magazines*
**homestore**.com – *shopping, style guide, "Hollywood decor"*
**improvenet**.com – *hire a contractor or do it yourself*
**inquisitivecook**.com – *special features including talk radio*
**myfooddirectory**.com – *recipes, ask the chef and more*
**ourhouse**.com – *furnish your home without even leaving it*
**outlawcook**.com – *quotations, fiction and cookbook reviews*
**purefood**.com – *buy materials for your organic garden*
**recipecenter**.com – *bookmark your favorites here*
**thaifoodandtravel**.com – *plan a meal and a vacation*
**theculinarysleuth**.com - *articles for cooks and food buffs*
**vegweb**.com – *free weekly newsletter with recipes*

# Money, Finance & Investing

Now here's an important topic that can mean the difference between a paycheck-to-paycheck existence and a life with some financial flexibility. We all know that it's important to make enough money to support ourselves, but what we do with our dollars is at least as important as how many dollars we have to begin with. Believe it or not, there are people who earn six figures and can barely pay the mortgage, while others with just mid-level incomes have savings accounts and investments and the freedom to travel now and then.

True poverty, of course, is a very different issue, but anyone who makes a living needs to know how to make their wages go as far as possible. And if you already have debts such as student loans, your need for money-management skills is even greater.

Although just the sound of terms such as "compound interest," "tax-deferred annuity," and "long-term fiscal growth" might make you queasy with confusion, the Internet has plenty of easy-to-follow guides, tutorials and tools to make sense of your personal finances. We present you, here, with a few to help you get going. The key is to begin your search with the most basic concepts – planning a monthly budget, for instance – and to move on to the next skill level only when you fully understand the first. Remember: this is something you're doing to help yourself, not to drive yourself crazy!

# bankrate.com

*Bankrate.com gives you tips on what to look for in a good bank, as well as comparisons between competitors.*

▶ An easy-to-use rate finder searches bank rates across the country by location or type of account.

▶ Articles keep you on top of the what's going on in the banking world.

▶ "The Dollar Diva" answers your financial questions.

# fool.com

*Authors of the best-selling Motley Fool investor's guides bring you daily investing advice with a humorous twist.*

▶ On-line investing seminars, books and even t-shirts are available on this fun and informative site.

▶ Find out which companies are currently hot and which are not.

▶ Track your own profile on-line.

# money.net

*Money.net is the home of the "Univer$ity of Money," which provides newcomers with the basics of investing.*

▶ Monitor your accounts and pay bills on-line.

▶ "Univer$ity of Money" breaks down into seven different categories such as "Investing Strategies."

▶ Stock market rates are provided.

Money, Finance & Investing

# netbank.com

*This on-line bank provides you with all the tools you need to open and update an account without ever leaving your home.*

▶ Advertises three times the average national interest rate.

▶ Pay bills on-line for free when you open a checking account.

▶ Offers on-line stock trading, mortgage loans and money market accounts.

# ourworld.compuserve.com/homepages/bonehead_finance

*Bonehead Finance uses the simplest terms to walk you through the world of personal finance; from establishing a budget to investing in stocks, bonds and mutual funds.*

▶ Provides tools for calculating a reasonable budget.

▶ Gives links to useful financial websites.

▶ On-site glossary explains terms and concepts.

▶ Sample budget gives explanations.

# paypal.com

*Paypal.com allows you to make on-line payments instantly to anyone who has an e-mail address.*

▶ Eliminate the need to wait for checks or money orders to clear after an auction.

▶ Opening an account is free!

▶ Send bills to those who owe you cash.

Money, Finance & Investing

# quicken.com

*A website for those who use the popular money-management software program called Quicken. The site allows you to pay your bills and file taxes on-line, track stock quotes and more.*

▶ Offers Quicken technical support.

▶ Search engines for general information and stock rates.

▶ Quicken software not required to use the website.

# smartmoney.com

*This site is filled with great tips on how to manage your personal finances, including college planning, debt management and estate planning.*

▶ Find out how much you could save under President Bush's tax plan.

▶ Use their worksheets to help you budget for big expenses like buying a house or saving for retirement.

▶ Give yourself a money makeover!

# stretcher.com

*The Dollar Stretcher, a weekly on-line magazine, focuses on living a good life while spending less.*

▶ Contains advice on paying back student loans.

▶ "My Best Bargain" section lets readers share tips on living frugally.

▶ Car specialist answers questions about fixing your automobile cheaply.

"The Dollar Stretcher" helps you save cash.

Money, Finance & Investing

# More Great Websites To Help You Save For A Rainy Day

Whether it's a rainy day or early retirement that you're saving for, these websites have everything from the latest investing news to tips on saving your loose change.

---

**ameritrade**.com – *trade on-line for a small fee*

**asec**.org – *American Savings Education Council savings tools*

**bplans**.com – *free sample business plans for entrepreneurs*

**cnbc**.com – *finance news from the television channel*

**consumercredit**.com – *non-profit credit counseling agency*

**credit**.com – *credit report request forms and debt counseling*

**datek**.com – *on-line trading with a "real time" ticker*

**fantasystockmarket**.com – *sign up and play for free*

**ft**.com – *Financial Times e-zine also comes in a UK version*

**investorguide**.com – *for both business and personal finance*

**kiplinger**.com – *business forecasts updated daily*

**nyse**.com – *the latest news from the New York Stock Exchange*

**pf101**.com – *their glossary is a great place for starters*

**quote**.com – *free Nasdaq information*

**siliconinvestor**.com – *market analysis and message boards*

**studentcredit**.com – *build up your good credit early*

**thestreet**.com – *calculators, economic calendars and more*

**wealtheffect**.com – *get your financial goals in order here*

**womensfinance**.com – *specialized site for women's finance*

**wsj**.com – *the on-line version of the Wall Street Journal*

**wsrn**.com – *Wall Street Research Net has the latest stock news*

**xe**.com/ucc – *converts currency into the latest rates*

Money, Finance & Investing

# Diet, Health & Fitness

What with all of the exciting possibilities in your post-graduation life, it's easy to forget one very important responsibility: the care and monitoring of your body. Gone are the days when your parents or coach kept track of your immunizations, eating habits and activity levels; now it's up to you to look after these things and to find a lifestyle that's healthy, wholesome and happy.

If you have no current health problems – great! Work to keep it that way by eating right, getting regular medical and dental care, and excercising in ways that are both useful and enjoyable. If you do have known health issues (diabetes, poor eyesight, or skin problems, for instance), then make it a policy to stay up-to-date on your condition, and to make self-care, medical treatment and lifestyle choices that will help you remain productive and well.

Many health and wellness websites exist which offer simple – even fun! – guidelines for pursuing a robust existence. Even if you're already active in caring for your body, you'll undoubtedly find inspiration in the articles, health news and fitness tips you'll find on-line. For those with specific medical conditions, some websites present in-depth coverage on everything from anemia to sports injuries to anorexia, and often have links to even more information. Whatever the case, your wellness is in your hands; so be a good mother to yourself!

## ama-assn.org

*The official home of the American Medical Association, this site is devoted to keeping patients and physicians up-to-date.*

▶ Get daily news and info on the latest developments in medicine.

▶ Find a specialist in your area using the site's "doctor finder."

▶ See which medical groups and hospitals provide the services you need.

## cbshealthwatch.com

*Get the latest reports on health that impact your daily life with this sub-site of medscape.com and CBS News.*

▶ Not sure exactly what the doctor prescribed for you? Check out meds in the drug directory.

▶ Sign up for "Mousecalls," the *cbshealthwatch.com* newsletter.

▶ Visit daily and read the ever-changing "Health Hint."

## cnn.com/health

*This site is jam-packed with pertinent news and pressing health issues from pollen counts to Alzheimer's disease.*

▶ Join discussion groups on topics such as AIDS, fitness and cloning.

▶ Multimedia resources are sure to entertain, as well as inform.

▶ Sign up for newsletters.

Diet, Health & Fitness

## cyberdiet.com

*If you're looking to lose weight or just begin eating healthier, check out cyberdiet.com for professional news and support.*

▸ Participate in live chat forums with professional doctors and nutritionists.

▸ Learn how to eat out, cook and otherwise plan healthy meals.

*Cyberdiet.com can show you how to eat right.*

## firstpath.com

*Are you in the market for fitness equipment? Firstpath.com will help you decide which programs and equipment are right for you.*

▸ Play "Fast Food Fight."

▸ Use their self-evaluation tools to find your weakest fitness areas.

▸ Read Dr. Kathy G. Wise's health column.

## fitnesslink.com

*Fitnesslink.com's goal is to help you "reshape your world." They'll show you the fitness plan that's right for you and give you tips on the best ways to boost your energy level.*

▸ Motivational ideas to psych you up for working out and getting healthy.

▸ Nutrition information and articles (on the site or in their newsletter).

▸ Find out the best ways to manage stress.

## fitnessonline.com

*Health isn't only about working out. Wellness is achieved through both mind and body.*

▶ Get your questions answered by Dr. Tim (resident M.D.), Nicole (pregnancy advisor) and Kathy Smith (fitness guru).

▶ Bodybuilding and general workout advice, like which fitness videos are the most effective.

▶ Nutrition and total body wellness information.

## healthanswers.com

*Whether you're just out of school, starting a family or taking care of an elderly family member, this site will walk you through the answers to all your health needs.*

▶ Consult their encyclopedia.

▶ Join in featured chats and general health discussions.

▶ Check out poison centers and other emergency information.

## healthatoz.com

*Healthatoz.com is a comprehensive site geared toward families.*

▶ Fun stuff to do like sending "Health E-cards," calculating your age potential and exchanging healthy recipes.

▶ Learn about breast cancer, how to eat healthy or even quit smoking.

▶ Find out how to make your home a safe environment.

Diet, Health & Fitness

## medscape.com

*Medscape Today focuses on medical conditions and news. Check them out if you're studying medicine or want detailed answers to common medical concerns.*

- Search their article database.
- They'll point you toward books on medical topics that interest you.
- Find information using their "patient resources" section.

## medterms.com

*Now and again, doctors use medical terms we just don't recognize. Use this on-line medical dictionary for explanations of conditions and medical terms.*

- Links to other health sites about everything from allergies to HIV.
- Shop their drugstore or fill a prescription on-line.
- Brush up on what to do in an emergency with their poison control and first aid guides.

## nal.usda.gov/fnic/foodcomp/Data/SR13/sr13.html

*This is the USDA's database of nutritional values.*

- Just plug in the name of a food and the search engine will pull up its full nutritional record; from vitamins and minerals to calories and fat and so on.
- Downloadable.
- Over 6,200 foods are listed – including possum!

Diet, Health & Fitness

## netsweat.com

*Don't be fooled by its cute name. This site will have you upping your workout resistance in no time!*

- ▸ Talk with their resident fitness trainer via e-mail.
- ▸ Use their fitness plans to create your own workout schedule.
- ▸ Thinking about becoming a fitness trainer? They'll tell you if you have what it takes!

## nutrition.org

*The Journal of Nutrition is a great place to find sound medical advice and breakthroughs in nutrition and health.*

- ▸ Get nutrient information for various foods.
- ▸ Subscribe to the *Journal* or sign up to receive a free sample issue.
- ▸ Stay informed by reading news updates and searching their database of articles.

## webmd.com

*A good general-purpose health site, webmd.com can help you find a doctor, locate health-related TV programs and plan a better lifestyle.*

- ▸ The "My Health Record" feature helps you keep all your medical info in one place.
- ▸ Quizzes let you evaluate your nutritional habits.
- ▸ Searchable database lists information on medical conditions, fitness and other issues.

Diet, Health & Fitness

# Surfin' For More Sites On Diet, Health & Fitness?

Staying fit and eating right is necessary for staying healthy. But if you've just graduated, chances are your lifestyle and fitness habits are going to change drastically. Spend some time on the 'net learning how to stay well.

**active**.com – *leagues and fitness advice for endurance sports*

**americanheart**.org – *heart-related, as well as general info*

**cancer**.org – *The American Cancer Society's website*

**dietitian**.com – *Q&A on subjects from alcohol to zinc*

**dietlinks**.com – *a helpful site on finding diet information*

**dietsite**.com – *diets, recipes, chat and sports nutrition info*

**dietwatch**.com – *join their community for diet support*

**healthfinder**.gov – *read news about national health issues*

**healthweb**.org – *a basic site listing health info by category*

**healthyideas**.com – *Prevention magazine's official website*

**hon**.ch – *this Swiss foundation is devoted to public health*

**ificinfo.health**.org – *International Food Information Council*

**mayohealth**.org – *find info on health from the Mayo Clinic*

**mentalhealth**.com – *mental wellness is necessary, too*

**naturalhealth1**.com – *read Natural Health magazine on-line*

**os.dhhs**.gov – *U.S. Department of Health and Human Services*

**parasolemt**.com/au/afa – *Parasol EMT's guide to first aid*

**plannedparenthood**.org – *read news and find local centers*

**reutershealth**.com – *international health-related news*

**rxlist**.com – *prescription, vitamin and alternative medicine*

**self**.com – *Self Magazine offers health and nutrition articles*

# Love & Relationships

After graduation, you no longer have a built-in opportunity to meet people who share your interests. Sure,

you see your co-workers on the job every day, but just because you work in the same place doesn't mean you have anything else in common. So what's a social being to do? Plenty of folks look in the yellow pages for churches, fitness clubs, or book groups where future friends may abound, and these are great ideas.

Internet buffs have favorite "places," as well, and you might do well to visit them. Chat rooms and discussion boards are on-line venues where people meet to discuss certain ideas (such as politics, music, cooking, etc.), or to gab with people in their age group, geographical location, and so on. On-line dating services are another option to help you meet like-minded individuals. Create your own ad or scan those that others have posted (many even include a photo) to find your Mr. or Mrs. Right.

The web is also a good place to look for advice on managing the relationships you already have. If you find yourself having difficulties with your significant other, chances are someone else has faced the same problem and written about it on-line. As the saying goes, two heads are better than one, and if you've run out of ideas on fixing your love life, don't give up until you've heard what others have to say about it.

# 1800student.com/cgi-bin/main_friends.cgi

*In the "CampusRomance" section of 1800Student.com, you can browse a directory of students to find your perfect match.*

- Search by age, sex or location.
- Ads include how important intelligence, outdoor activities, humor, sex and diet and fitness are to each potential date.
- Even though the site is designed for students, professionals are also listed.

# americansingles.com

*One of the most popular dating sites on the 'net, American Singles has been bringing couples together throughout the country for years.*

- Membership is free.
- Take a tour of the site before signing up for the service.
- Over 3 million members have joined so far.

# clubs.yahoo.com

*Similar to chat rooms, Yahoo's clubs are special-interest discussion groups created by members. Membership is free and you're welcome to create your own club.*

- Club topics cover everything from movies to finance to pets.
- "The Clubhouse" showcases new clubs every Tuesday.
- Create a private, unlisted club for you and your friends.

Love & Relationships

# **datingfun**.com

*Datingfun.com is "your complete dating resource." The site has everything you need, "from pick-up to break-up."*

▸ Study the "Pick-Up Lines" section to help you meet someone new and then take a look at the "Date Ideas" for somewhere to go.

▸ Find out which phase of the "Dating Timeline" you are in.

▸ Impress friends (and dates!) with trivia you learned from the "Dating Trivia" section.

# **effectiveliving**.com

*Relationship expert Bill Ferguson has helped millions of couples rekindle the love they almost lost.*

▸ Learn how to build a better relationship.

▸ Sign up for either a workshop or for individual counseling.

▸ Buy books and tapes on-line for even more help.

# **excite**.com/communities/chat/

*Choose either "Excite Chat" (which requires a download but has more features) or "Chat Lite" (no download, but limited options).*

▸ *Excite.com*'s voice feature works like an on-line phone.

▸ Downloadable "avators" let you represent your on-line personality with an icon.

▸ Lists popular chat rooms.

Love & Relationships

## geekcheck.com

*This site promises "dating advice for the criminally insane" and delivers useful tongue-in-cheek ideas for improving your love life.*

▶ Read high school horror stories, a collection of horrendous personal ads and more.

▶ Has both silly and sweet advice.

▶ Check out the "Bachelor and Bachelorette of the Week."

Brenda from *www.geekcheck.com*.

## ivillage.com/relationships

*This women's site is more like an on-line magazine, featuring articles, quizzes and tips on keeping your relationships happy and healthy.*

▶ Think your dating life is bad? Read the "Worst Date of the Week" and think again!

▶ Have your questions answered by "Mr. Answer Man."

▶ Find out how to put the passion back into your relationship – and keep it there for good!

## lovesites.com

*This is a comprehensive directory of chat, dating and personals sites on the Internet.*

▶ Directory is divided into several categories and each link is followed by a short description.

▶ Alternative, international and religious sites are also listed.

52  Love & Relationships

# lovingyou.com

*Lovingyou.com advertises that it is "your community for everything you need to get, fall and stay in love."*

- Check out helpful articles such as "20 Date Ideas Under $20" in the "Dating" section.
- Get free "Love Tips" delivered directly to your inbox.
- Explore one of the many communities on the site.

# match.com

*Over 4 million visitors have used this dating site. With that kind of audience, you're sure to meet someone you connect with!*

- Searching the site's databases is free.
- Read the "Love Letters" of successfully matched couples.
- Check out some "Conversation Starters" to help you avoid those awkward silences.

# relationshipweb.com

*"First aid for relationships,"* plus discussion groups on love, marriage, divorce, abuse and emotional issues.

- Thousands of related links.
- "Daily Relationship Readings," searchable by calendar date or subject.
- Check out old forums in their archives which are categorized by subject.

Love & Relationships

# talkcity.com

*Talkcity.com offers discussions, articles and clubs, as well as chat rooms for people of all ages and interests.*

▶ Choose to chat about a specific topic or with a specific group of people.

▶ Give your input on the "Hot Topic" of the day.

▶ Sit in on live chats with celebrities or read transcripts of past events.

# virtualkiss.com

*Before you go on your next date, you might want to check out this site, which gives you advice, quizzes and stories. There's even a kissing school!*

▶ Enter a "kissing contest," buy some stuff, or cut out some "kissing coupons" and present them to your honey.

▶ Find out your compatibility in the astrology section.

▶ Send a virtual kiss to someone from the "E-Kissing Booth."

# whodoyoulove.com

*This fun site is filled with everything love-related; from e-cards and chat to a live "LoveCam."*

▶ Julia London, "the first lady of romance," answers your love questions.

▶ Love translations help you learn how to speak the international language.

54  Love & Relationships

# And Here's More On Love & Relationships

Whether you're already in a relationship and need some advice or are a swinging single and in search of a date (or even just someone to chat with), these sites are sure to have something for you.

**astromate**.com – *uses astrology help you score a sweetie*

**breakupgirl**.com – *"saving love lives the world over"*

**coolchannel**.com – *chat, e-mail, forums, games and more*

**cyberlove**.net – *on-line talk show about relationships*

**dateable**.com – *everything you need to get started in love*

**datingclub**.com – *also in Spanish, German and Italian*

**dumped-online**.com – *for the "dumpee" and "dumper" alike*

**flirt**.com – *this romance channel has advice and celebrities*

**friendfinder**.com – *find a mate with this on-line service*

**friends-lovers**.com – *an on-line magazine for everyone*

**getromantic**.com – *articles, forums and a gift-giving guide*

**love-4-life**.com – *chat, find love or browse the bookstore*

**love.freewire**.co.uk – *a list of dating sites for those 18+*

**loveandlearn**.com – *ask the panel your love questions*

**lovecalculator**.com – *does you + them = love?*

**lovestories**.com – *a book club, personals and much more*

**passionup**.com – *send a letter, poem or e-card to loved ones*

**people2people**.com – *features include video and voice*

**relationship-talk**.com – *on love, dating and relationships*

**rom101**.com – *get on their daily inspiration mailing list*

**theglobe**.com – *join a club, scan personals or play games*

**worlddatingchannel**.com – *personals from around the globe*

# Going Out On The Town

One of the great things about the Internet is that it can give you ideas you'd never have thought of on your own. Take the topic of nighttime entertainment, for example. The first things which spring to your mind are probably movies, bars or nightclubs – and for sure, the 'net has plenty of pages with showtimes and club info – but if you surf some hot Internet  ticketing spots, your options expand to include stand-up comedy shows, theater productions, concerts of all types and even special museum exhibits.

Often, when you visit these sites, you can get detailed information on what you'll find at each venue – sort of like an on-line brochure – and then you also have the option of buying your tickets while you're on-line. What an easy way to book your evening! Plus, you can even e-mail your confirmation to friends so there won't be any confusion about who was supposed to be where, when!

For those times when you do want "the usual," entertainment websites can give you film reviews and ratings; lists of what's playing at specific theaters; and tell you what's coming soon to the silver screen. Many bars and clubs now have their own websites as well and you can browse directories to find some of the exciting possibilities near you. If you're traveling, remember to check for nightlife in your destination city before you go – you just might miss out if you don't do your homework!

# americantheaterweb.com

*Movies and concerts aren't the only type of entertainment out there for nightlife seekers. In big cities and small communities alike, theater is alive and well.*

▶ Look up show information by region and customize the page for future information.

▶ Shop their store for all your theater-related needs.

▶ Sign up for their free newsletter.

# beertravelers.com

*A state-by-state list of microbreweries helps you find local hang-out spots, as well as great beer.*

▶ Irish, German, and English brewpubs listed, as well as those in all 50 states.

▶ Top microbreweries are rated and discussed.

▶ Suggests good adventures and pub crawls.

# cityhits.com

*Just select a city from their database and you can plan a dream date or a night out on the town with friends.*

▶ Find out what there is to do in a city you're visiting for the first time.

▶ Know whether you'll need sunblock or a rain coat using their five-day weather forecast.

Going Out On The Town

## clubplanet.com

*Everything you ever wanted to know about "nightlifestyle" is on this vibrant site devoted to clubbing and barhopping.*

▶ Check out the site for your daily dose of "Nightlifestyle News."

▶ Find a club or bar in your area.

▶ Read the site editors' top club picks and enter wild contests.

## comedycalendar.com

*If you're in the mood for a good laugh, check out this national listings of comedy clubs and comedians near you.*

▶ Search for local comedy clubs, talent agencies and upcoming shows in your area.

▶ Read the "Daily Funnies" and shop their store.

▶ View "Reel Reviews" and get to know today's hottest comics through celebrity interviews.

## cuisinenet.com

*This restaurant guide lists eateries in over 12,000 cities.*

▶ Search for restaurants by cuisine, price range, location, amenities or any combination of the four.

▶ See menus before even leaving home.

▶ Not sure what you're in the mood for? Check out the site's top picks for your city.

## enspot.com

*By simply entering a zip code or local metro area, you will be given information on all sorts of events happening right in your own backyard.*

▶ Register with the site to access personalized event promotions and discounts.

▶ The site includes less conventional activities such as festivals, trade shows and video releases.

## events.excite.com

*Search for ticketed events in concerts, sports and performing arts categories. Plug in your zip code and local events will be displayed every time you visit the page.*

▶ "Places to Go" category also suggests non-performance activities, such as the Exotic Erotic Ball in San Francisco.

▶ Buy tickets on-line.

▶ "Invite a Friend" lets you e-mail event details to others.

## heyblanch.com

*BLANCH is the Bar, Lounge And Nightclub Cyber Homepage and aspires to list every night spot on the planet which has its own homepage.*

▶ Includes listings for cybercafes.

▶ Searchable by continent, country and state.

▶ Gives address, phone, e-mail and website information.

Going Out On The Town

# nightclubs.com

*Subtitled "Your Information Source For Nightclubs Around The World," nightclubs.com's comprehensive site will never leave you without a destination!*

- Search for nightclubs in every country or in your own backyard.

- Read about club events and club happenings on their front page.

- Become a site member to add or revise club information.

# playbill.com

*Playbill.com will keep you up to date on which shows are worthwhile and which thespians are hot.*

- Get seating charts for major venues.

- Show summaries, ticket prices and availability listed for Broadway, Off-Broadway, Regional and London tours.

- Read celebrity interviews and search job postings for performers and backstage staff.

# pollstar.com

*Pollstar is "The Concert Hotwire." Search for shows by artist, venue or city.*

- Tap into their archives and Top 50 for trips down memory lane.

- Browse listings of the hot nationwide tours in progress.

- Read up-to-the-minute news about your favorite artists.

Going Out On The Town

# Where Else To Go Before You Go Out

Check out these Internet sites for solutions to cabin fever, how to throw the perfect party and painting the town red with budgeted funds.

---

**casinocity**.com – *finding a good casino is no longer a gamble*

**clubthings**.com – *your Internet shopping spot for club gear*

**culturefinder**.com – *check out arts events nationwide*

**dine4less**.com – *the place to look when dining on a budget*

**eventguide**.com – *daily and annual event calendars*

**findthefun**.com – *sports, music and movies listed by state*

**getouttoday**.com – *nightlife and event finder for all ages*

**mojam**.com – *what tours are hot and where to catch them*

**nightclub**.com – *browse the regional "club connection" page*

**nightclubs**.net – *look for clubs or chat with club-goers*

**nightguide**.net – *portal site for local and international spots*

**ontap**.com/bar – *play bartender at your next party*

**party411**.com – *plan everything from birthday to toga parties*

**realbeer**.com – *find local brew pubs and microbreweries*

**sfx**.com – *see music, theater, sports and comedy show listings*

**smartpages**.com – *visit Smartpages' national city guides*

**theatre**.com – *check out their deals on "last-minute tickets"*

**theatredb**.com – *search events by show, person or venue*

**tickets**.com – *get national entertainment news and tickets*

**ticketmaster**.com – *search for events and buy tickets*

**webtender**.com – *drink recipes, random drink suggestions*

**wwevents**.com – *events in America, Europe and Australia*

# Movies, Music & More . . .

Ah, independence! Your free time is yours to spend as you like, without anyone monitoring your TV habits, reading material or musical taste. If you want to stay up until 4 a.m. finishing that detective novel (and arrive bleary-eyed at work in the morning!) no one's going to stop you. If you have a secret addiction to soaps, so much that you tape them to watch in the evenings, no one needs to know. You now have the freedom to entertain yourself as you choose!

But what is freedom, if you don't have the tools to make the most of it? A bookworm needs the reviews and publication dates to help them know when something they would like to read is going to become available – so, for that matter, do music buffs, TV-a-holics, and video addicts. Well, it's web pages to the rescue – everything you ever wanted to know about the entertainment industry can be found on-line, including some of the entertainment itself! Plus, there's no better way to fulfill your entertainment shopping needs: can't wait to get your hands on that hot new cd? Many sites will let you "pre-order" future releases, so all you have to do is sit back and wait for your much anticipated merchandise to arrive.

This chapter covers sites that will give you info on books; magazines; music; TV; movies; and more; plus supply all of the celebrity news and gossip you crave. Additionally, some of these sites have chat rooms where you can exchange opinions and ideas with other people who watch, read or listen to the same things you do!

## **bookwire**.com

*Find everything about books on this comprehensive site: best-seller lists, daily book reviews, author appearances and even links to agents and publishers!*

▶ Suggested links include *Boston Book Review* and *Publisher's Weekly*.

▶ Calendar cites information on writers' conferences and workshops.

## **eonline**.com

*Billed as "entertainment's home page," E! Online is your source for news and gossip as well as music and movie info.*

▶ Tons of photos track the stars and their foibles.

▶ Movie reviews help you choose what to see – or not to see.

▶ Info on awards shows and other glitzy parties give the inside scoop on Tinseltown.

▶ On-line contests offer chances to win cool stuff.

## **half**.com

*This site allows you to buy or sell previously owned books, music, movies, or video games for a fixed price.*

▶ "Wish List" feature lets you ask to be notified if an item you're looking for goes up for sale.

▶ "Bargain Bin" lists books for under $.99 and CDs for under $2.99.

Movies, Music & More . . .

# hollywood.com

*Before you plan a night out at the movies, check out hollywood.com for showtimes, movie reviews and other necessary tidbits to enhance your movie-going experience.*

▶ Watch clips of hot Hollywood events, movie trailers and interviews with the stars.

▶ Read movie reviews for most feature-length, short and independent films.

▶ Get showtimes for theaters in your hometown.

# live-online.com

*This directory of on-line musical events, cybercasts and chats is one of the largest music sites on the web.*

▶ "Digital Jukebox" has weekly downloadable singles.

▶ Special "Left of the Dial" section provides links to the best radio stations on the web.

# museumtix.com

*With listings to virtually every major American museum, this site offers ticket sales, descriptions of the events and a list of the most popular on-going events.*

▶ Lists events by categories: historical, Impressionist, etc.

▶ Suggests events happening today, for spur-of-the-moment eventgoers.

▶ This site also lists info on other related events, such as whale watches at the New England Aquarium.

Movies, Music & More . . .

## nytimes.com/books

*The official site of the New York Times Book Review gives info on the latest best-sellers and their authors.*

▸ Has audio links to author interviews and readings.

▸ "First Chapters" section gives sneak previews of books you might want to read.

▸ Forums and on-line reading groups help connect you to other readers.

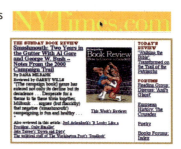

## ratingzone.com

*This interesting website predicts what movies, books and music you'll like based upon a quiz you fill out.*

▸ Supports Internet Explorer and Netscape.

▸ Two types of guides are offered; "Quick Picks" leads to a short survey which gives you eight recommendations.

▸ The more in-depth "Precision Guide" actually suggests what type of music you'll like and gives dozens of suggestions.

## realityblurred.com

*A cyberindex of reality TV shows like Survivor and Temptation Island, Reality Blurred gives showtimes, synopses and reviews.*

▸ Gossipy articles reveal behind-the-scenes facts and fiction about the shows.

▸ Searchable archives let you access past issues.

Movies, Music & More . . .

## salon.com

*An on-line magazine, salon.com has articles and commentary on the arts, politics, business, lifestyles and more. Chat rooms on various subjects attract people of all types.*

▸ On-line chat groups cover hot topics of today.

▸ Audio section features a new item each issue; recently, Kurt Vonnegut could be heard reading *Slaughterhouse Five*.

▸ "Table Talk" section allows readers to start a new subject or participate in an ongoing one.

## theatlantic.com

*The on-line version of Atlantic Monthly magazine has everything the print version does, except paper waste!*

▸ Searchable archive lets you read back issues.

▸ Magazine topics include books and criticism, politics, food, fiction, travel and more.

▸ E-mail feature will send copies of an article to a friend.

## tvguide.com

*Want to keep track of your favorite shows? The on-line version of TV Guide follows all channels nationwide.*

▸ Listings sortable by show type – sports, soaps, etc.

▸ Entertaining articles talk about shows, stars and celebrity news.

▸ On-line store has TV collectible merchandise.

Movies, Music & More . . .

# Keeping You Entertained

Looking for something entertaining to do? Visit the following sites for a little direction in your Internet surfing.

abebooks.com – *search for rare or out-of-print books*
artnet.com – *Artnet magazine's guide to art events and news*
artswire.com – *arts news, workshops and tutorials*
authorsontheweb.com – *articles on writing and writers*
billboard.com – *watch your favorite artists climb the charts*
cbs.com/lateshow – *read Letterman's "Late Show Top Ten"*
cybereditions.com – *turns out-of-print books into e-books*
fandom.com – *news and other stuff for fantasy enthusiasts*
hugedisk.com – *a men's humor e-zine "so manly it sweats"*
imdb.com – *database of both current and classic movies*
katrillion.com – *movies, music, sports, games and contests*
mcsweeneys.net – *daily humor and slice-of-life observations*
modernhumorist.com – *devoted to pop culture humor*
mp3.com – *download music, send e-cards and more*
mrshowbiz.com – *articles and reviews on your favorite stars*
mtv.com – *news, reviews, downloads and MTV show info*
music.com – *download, shop or read industry news*
napster.com – *download thousands of songs and sound bytes*
newpages.com – *'net portal to the best independent media*
plastic.com – *all the quirkiest stories on the 'net*
poets.org – *lists events and news on the poetry scene*
suck.com – *a humor magazine updated every weekday*
thecelebritycafe.com – *celebrity interviews and contests*
womanrock.com – *all the info you need on women who rock*

Movies, Music & More . . .

# Travel

Sometimes, it's true, you've just got to get away from it all – just exit your life for a while and see someplace different. Escapism is a fine reason to travel, but of course there are others – education, social enlightenment, and self-discovery, just to name a few. As a person on a budget (and who isn't, besides Bill Gates?), you have to make your travel plans carefully, hoping to get as much vacationing as you can, for as little money as possible.

It helps to be open-minded about your definitions of "travel" and "vacation," because your best deals may not be of the airplane-hotel-rental-car variety. Budget travelers surfing the web can find, for instance, great bargains on backpacking vacations or hippie-style bus tours. Cheap airfares show up from time to time and if you combine one with a Eurail train pass, you might see all of Europe while never paying for lodging (just sleep on the train).

As always, the key idea to using the Internet to your advantage is research, research, research. Several of the budget travel websites we list here will send you new vacation-on-a-shoestring updates or newsletters at no cost as they become available. Others have print catalogs to which you can subscribe, or forums where you can learn about other people's experiences (both good and bad) with different vendors, locations, and the like.

## fodors.com

*The home of Fodor's Travel Publications, fodors.com is a great place to find out where to buy the best coffee in Europe or how to travel on a budget.*

▶ Vacation how-tos.

▶ Business travel info.

▶ Create a "Miniguide" by plugging in your trip info.

## frommers.com

*Designed with the budget traveler in mind, this site has up-to-date info on airfare, hotels, car rentals and more.*

▶ Search engines allow you to look for hotels, restaurants, shopping and entertainment anywhere.

▶ "Hot Spot of the Month" lets you enter to win vacations.

▶ "Road Trips" section offers advice on travelling by car.

▶ Letters to the editor feature readers' recommendations – and warnings – on travel-related topics.

## greentortoise.com

*Want to take a road trip, but don't have a car? Consider travelling on a bunk-bed-filled tour bus.*

▶ Buses stop at points on the way for local activities.

▶ Last-minute specials offer discounted travel.

▶ Destinations include Alaska, Baja, Death Valley, Grand Canyon and more.

Travel

# letsgo.com

*Letsgo.com is run entirely by students who travel the world and then tell you how to follow in their footsteps.*

- ▶ Travel on a budget using their directories and guides to currency and other tools necessary for world exploration.

- ▶ Find a travel buddy, a hostel or just talk about your travel adventures in the forum.

- ▶ View video clips.

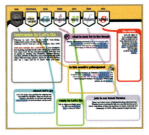

# priceline.com

*If you're not picky about which airline you travel on, or the time or length of your flight, this is a great way to travel for less.*

- ▶ Decide where and when you want to travel and offer a dollar amount. Priceline will automatically check for an airline willing to sell you a ticket at that price.

- ▶ Also offers lodging and car rental services.

- ▶ Be warned that you will be billed for the ticket without being asked if the itinerary is acceptable.

# thebackpacker.net

*If you're interested in seeing Europe on foot, you'll find all the advice you need here.*

- ▶ Search engine lists hostels in Europe and elsewhere.

- ▶ Tips on rail passes, cheap airfare, budgeting and more.

- ▶ "Beer Index" features the best beers worldwide.

# Travel Over To These Sites For More Great Vacation Information

Don't settle for the traditional Spring Break in Cancun – check out these sites for adventure, R&R and price breaks.

---

**bestfares**.com – *everything from ski trips to Caribbean cruises*

**cheaptickets**.com – *discount flights, cruises, rooms and cars*

**counciltravel**.com – *student travel resources and itineraries*

**crazydogtravel**.com – *news and tips for safe backpacking*

**economytravel**.com – *low international rates and planning*

**emsonline**.com – *buy gear for your outdoor activities*

**eurorailways**.com – *information on seeing Europe by rail*

**gorp**.com – *find adventure activities and vacation planners*

**inyourpocket**.com – *check out their series of handy guides*

**lonelyplanet**.com – *postcards, guides and travel highlights*

**nationalgeographic**.com – *see the world on your computer*

**onetravel**.com – *travel deals, discounts and an advisor*

**ricksteves**.com – *Europe "Through the Back Door" with Rick*

**roughguides**.com – *travel reference guides and other news*

**smarterliving**.com/student – *price breaks for student travel*

**thetraveldoctor**.com – *get medical info before you leave*

**ticketplanet**.com – *book flights, hotels, cars and more*

**travelocity**.com – *a complete resource site for travel planning*

**travelroads**.com – *search destinations and get discounts*

**ulyssesguides**.com – *buy guides and read their newsletter*

**undergroundtravel**.com – *travel passes, videos and news*

**whatsgoingon**.com – *find worldwide adventure and events*

**worldsurface**.com – *travelers discuss their adventures*

# Style, Fashion & Beauty

Take a closet full of clothes, throw in some cosmetics or a blow dryer, add a dash of hair gel, and what have you got? Personal style. Wherever your style originated (classmates, magazine ads, window displays), it's sure to evolve over time and, if keeping track of that development is important to you, some helpful resources are in order. With that in mind, the following websites may come in handy.

Some of the links which follow are general-purpose sites, covering the whole gamut of fashion, beauty and style. In them, you'll find hints and tips for creating your own "look;" plus discussion boards, articles on the latest trends, celebrity news, and plenty of products for sale. Other sites are more specific, focussing on just one aspect of style (hair, for example), or simply listing links to a whole lot of other sites with fashion-related info.

If you already know what you want and simply need to pick it up, the web is a great place to shop – it saves you travel time, while shielding you from those overzealous sales clerks at the makeup counter! When shopping for personal care products on-line, however, make sure you familiarize yourself with the site's return policy: many sites will only accept returns on unopened products. And as with all on-line purchases, make sure the retailer you choose has a secure server – one which encrypts your credit card information so it's not intercepted by anyone else.

## beauty.com

*This site not only offers several different product lines for purchase, but it has some great information, too!*

▶ Makeup artist Kevyn Aucoin shows off his talent by doing a new makeover each month.

▶ Michael Edwards answers all of your fragrance questions.

▶ Special products are designed exclusively for *beauty.com* customers.

## beautybuzz.com

*This site is updated daily with the latest fashion, makeup, skin care, fragrance and hair news.*

▶ The "World Wide Shopping Directory" lists the best shops around the world.

▶ Read interviews from industry experts.

▶ Find a spa to help you relax.

## beautynet.com

*Billed as "the virtual salon for beauty, wellness and style," beautynet.com features tips on hair, skin and nail care.*

▶ Image bank displays sample hair, makeup and nail styles.

▶ Find salons in your area.

▶ News articles keep you up-to-date on what's hot right now.

Style, Fashion & Beauty

## fashionangel.com

*Providing links to fashion-related websites, Fashion Angel covers alternative fashion, top designers, vintage clothes, on-line 'zines and more.*

▸ Includes shopping sites and merchandise links.

▸ Rates the best sites.

▸ Some links lead you to used designer duds.

## fashionmall.com

*A shopper's paradise, fashionmall.com will wow you with its limitless options and great prices on name-brand fashions.*

▸ Shop by "department," "floor" or search for a specific brand.

▸ Aside from clothes, *fashionmall.com* also offers accessories, jewelry, beauty products and home goods.

▸ Check out the site's "Deal of the Day."

## ftv.com

*Straight from Paris, ftv.com is the broadcast site of Fashion TV.*

▸ Watch video footage from fashion shows.

▸ "Mens Only" area highlights menswear designers, while the "Lingerie" section highlights . . . well, you know . . .

▸ Listen to FTV music.

▸ Find out models' birthdays.

# hairboutique.com

*Dedicated to hair styles and hair care, this site has an image gallery of trends; plus hair-related news, links and a message board where visitors can exchange tips.*

- "JerkyFlea's Celebrity Hair Spray" gives you the details on the latest hair styles in Hollywood.
- Recent articles discussed straightening hair, finding a great colorist and possible links between cancer and hair dyes.
- Their "Hair-o-scope" predicts your good hair days for the month.

# hintmag.com

*An on-line fashion 'zine for those who like to follow the trends, hintmag.com supplies the latest in fashion news.*

- Video links provide glimpses of runway shows, backstage action and designer interviews.
- Up-and-coming fashion models are rated and discussed.
- "Chic Happens," a monthly column, provides fashion news and gossip.

# instyle.com

*The on-line version of InStyle magazine has just as much great information as the print version.*

- Discover celebrities' favorite beauty secrets.
- Get beauty and fashion advice from the experts.

**Style, Fashion & Beauty**

## makeupdiva.com

*This site allows you to "Ask The Makeup Diva" all of your questions about beauty and cosmetics.*

- Subscribe to her newsletter so you never miss the "Diva's" advice or search past columns to find the answers you're looking for.

- Offers links to beauty shops, magazines and other sites.

## style.com

*Style.com is the on-line home of Vogue and W magazines. Their site is a great source of fashion news and insider info.*

- Find out the hottest looks for the upcoming season.

- Explore the "People & Parties" section to discover who is wearing what this year.

- Take a look at the hottest fashion designers.

## thelipstickpage.com

*Updated daily, this site has everything that you've ever wanted to know about lipstick.*

- Find out which brands and colors the celebrities swear by.

- "The Lipstick Page Hang Out" provides advice from readers on their favorite products.

- Search the "Lipstick Library" database for specific brands and shades.

# Here's More To Help You Increase Your Style Quotient

The world of fashion and beauty is always changing. Keep up with the latest styles and beauty advances with these websites.

**allure**.com – *everything you need to look your very best*

**beautycafe**.com – *shop here for all of your beauty needs*

**beautylink**.com – *columnists answer all of your questions*

**boo**.com – *shop "bootiques" or become a "style scout"*

**dressforsuccess**.com – *buy the video or get tips on menswear*

**emakemeup**.com – *make-up and cosmetic reviews*

**fashion-planet**.com – *fashion news in an on-line 'zine*

**fashionclick**.com – *the world of fashion at your fingertips*

**fashionlive**.com – *the newest styles straight from the catwalk*

**firstview**.com – *virtual tour of NY Fashion Week and more*

**girlshop**.com – *hip clothing and a "guyshop," too*

**greatdayamerica**.com/style – *tips for both men and women*

**healthnbeauty**.com – *beauty products put to the test*

**icompact**.com – *chat, message boards and how-to tips*

**jbtrends**.com – *latest fashion trends for women aged 15-25*

**makeupalley**.com – *all-occasion beauty tips and a directory*

**planetpretty**.com – *beauty news and celebrity gossip, too*

**style-and-fashion**.com – *"the independent fashion network"*

**styledetective**.com – *predicting the styles of tomorrow*

**thebodyshop**.com – *all-natural beauty products for sale*

**visual-makeover**.com – *hair care, sample styles and advice*

**worldwidebeautystore**.com – *makeup, skin care and more*

Style, Fashion & Beauty

# Shopping Sites

A well-managed personal budget need not prohibit the occasional fun purchase; it should just make you careful to shop for the best deals on what you need. In the past, you'd have to wait for clearance sales at your favorite stores before buying anything, but we're in the Internet age now: every day is a sale day!

Many name-brand retailers offer web catalogs, most of which have links to clearance merchandise – everything from bath products to furniture. If you have a particular favorite (J. Crew, Eddie Bauer, etc.), see if it has an on-line catalog; chances are you'll find a sale category in the index. Some sites even offer "web specials" – sale prices available only to customers who order on-line. It costs a company much less to take a "cyber order," after all, than to pay a sales clerk to stand in a store.

Then there are websites in which everything is offered at a big discount – these are often the equivalents of fire sales or going-out-of-business liquidators and it's not unheard of for goods to be discounted as much as 75%. And don't neglect on-line auctions as places to get terrific bargains. If you know what you want, and what it would cost in a store, it's a good idea to see if someone is auctioning it – new or used – for less. Be aware that shipping charges will add to the purchase price, but most auction listings tell you up front what it will cost to ship your item.

## amazon.com

*Originally a bookstore, amazon.com now offers just about everything entertainment-related.*

▶ Both books and shipping costs are offered at discounts.

▶ Purchase DVDs, CDs, VHS, toys and software.

▶ Send free e-cards and download music.

## carday.com

*You can browse used cars for sale by dealers or private owners, then make an offer on-line. If your offer is accepted, you can even test drive the vehicle before purchasing.*

▶ All cars are certified used vehicles – those which have been inspected and evaluated by a qualified facility.

▶ Includes fleet cars (those that have been previously owned by corporations) for sale.

▶ All cars have at least a 6-month warranty.

## carpoint.msn.com

*Just about everything you need to know about car shopping can be found here, from advice columns to reviews of new models by automotive experts.*

▶ Find the trade-in value of any car through the *Kelley Blue Book*.

▶ Browse new and used car classified ads.

▶ Info on recalls, traffic reports and more.

## ebay.com

*The world's largest on-line auction site has millions of items up for sale at any given time. If you can't find it anywhere else, chances are someone is auctioning it on eBay.*

- Hundreds of auction categories are here, from automobiles to collectibles.

- Registration is free and allows you to buy or sell on the site.

- Each buyer and seller gets customer reviews after transactions, which are accessible through the site.

## iloveadeal.com

*Whether you need a bracelet or a breadmaker, you're sure to find it on this clearance shopping site.*

- Merchandise categories include: "Jewelry;" "Art and More;" "For the Home;" "Apparel" and "Entertainment."

- Blowout section lists a wide variety of items at rock-bottom prices.

## mcphee.com

*"Outfitters of Popular Culture," Archie McPhee is the place to get anything from a glow-in-the-dark alien to a purse in the shape of an armadillo.*

- Order their print catalog.

- "Cult of McPhee" e-mail newsletter keeps you in touch.

- On-line contests let you win gift certificates and cool "toys."

## overstock.com

*The Internet version of a liquidation center, overstock.com has an ever-changing array of new merchandise at up to 70% off store prices.*

▶ You can search by brand name or ask to see new arrivals.

▶ Products listed by department, including apparel, luggage, sports gear and more.

▶ E-mail newsletter sends hot deals to your inbox.

## pcmall.com

*If you're looking for computer goodies, keep your eyes on pcmall.com.*

▶ Get personalized recommendations to suit your needs.

▶ Purchase best-selling items at discount prices.

▶ "Resources" section offers financing and product support.

## powells.com

*Powell's sells both new and used books, which means you can save money while finding those out-of-print items you've been searching for.*

▶ Browse books by genre.

▶ Enter to win free books.

▶ "Author Interviews" section features talks with both well-known and lesser-known writers.

## Keep On Shoppin'

Shopping the Internet can save you time and is a great way to save money, too.

**allposters**.com – *decorate in style with art prints and posters*

**bluefly**.com – *buy designer clothes for less*

**bluenile**.com – *browse and purchase jewelry hassle-free*

**bn**.com – *preview and buy books from Barnes & Noble*

**cdnow**.com – *purchase music, collectibles and accessories*

**classifieds2000**.com – *search all categories of classified ads*

**coolsavings**.com – *download coupons for your favorite stores*

**dailyedeals**.com – *hot deals and coupons for popular e-tailers*

**delias**.com – *fun and funky clothes at great prices*

**eastbay**.com – *sports and athletic apparel for him or her*

**egghead**.com – *computers and accessories at great prices*

**emusic**.com – *buy MP3s for about $1 a song, $9 an album*

**esmarts**.com – *coupons, reward programs and newsletters*

**flooz**.com – *buy virtual gift certificates to multiple e-tailers*

**gap**.com – *The Gap advertises "hassle-free on-line shopping"*

**jcrew**.com – *shop the entire catalog and the clearance rack*

**mysimon**.com – *comparison shop for the best 'net prices*

**netgrocer**.com – *save time by grocery shopping from home*

**outpost**.com – *computers and other fun gadgets for sale*

**sale**.com – *find the best sales at major stores and e-tailers*

**urbanmall**.com – *discounted urban-esque apparel*

**videoflicks**.com – *DVDs and VHS at blowout prices*

**walmart**.com – *shop the discount department store on-line*

**walnutacres**.com – *buy all kinds of organic food on-line*

# Sites To Help You Simplify Your Life

A few years ago, a man made headlines when he agreed to stay in his house for a year – never leaving the comfort of his home for any reason! So, you may wonder, how exactly did he get anything done? The man in question used technology to his advantage and decided to conduct his entire life via the Internet. Using his computer as his only means of communication, he could fill prescriptions, buy stamps and even perform his job.

Now, no one is suggesting you become a hermit, but your life can be a little easier if you do, on-line, some of the errands you once had to make a special trip out of the house to accomplish. New web-based services are popping up all the time – you can now rent videos, send faxes and even make phone calls on-line! So, if there's something you never had time to do, or if you're looking to simplify your life to have time for the things that you truly enjoy, go ahead and click away.

But that's not all! In addition to providing direct services, the Internet is filled with sites to help you make your daily life a little easier. Whatever you need to find, chances are that it is somewhere on the 'net. Maps and directions; yellow pages; and even reminder services and address books are all at your fingertips so that you never forget another important name, number or date again!

# efax.com

*If you don't have your own fax machine, you can still receive faxes – by e-mail!*

- Signing up is free.
- Also lets you receive voice mail.
- Note that you may be assigned a fax number outside your area code – which would result in long-distance fees.

# headlinespot.com

*Why go to one news site when you can access them all through one website? Headlinespot.com brings you all of the latest headlines and news in one place.*

- Search news stories by region, subject or media.
- "Today's Top Stories" provides headlines which are continuously updated throughout the day.
- Check crosswords, horoscopes, humor and lottery sections.

# mapblast.com

*Map out your route before you even leave the house. Just type in your destination and where you're coming from for a detailed map of the shortest (or fastest) way to get there.*

- Locate restaurants, hotels and FedEx stops on your route.
- Offers discounts on hotels and car rentals.
- Wireless services allow you to take *mapblast.com* with you on your trips for easy reference.

**84** Sites To Help You Simplify Your Life

## rx.com

*Rx.com provides one-stop pharmacy shopping. You can read the latest health news, pick up items and even fill prescriptions!*

▸ Create an account for customized service every time you log on.

▸ A pharmacist is always on-line to answer your questions.

▸ A "Reference Desk" helps you look up information about health conditions, drugs and natural medicines.

## usps.com

*This is the official website of the U.S. Postal Service.*

▸ Lists postage rates and sells stamps by mail.

▸ Delivery confirmation is available to make sure your packages arrived safely.

▸ The site even provides a program which lets you print postage on your PC!

## yellowpages.com

*In need of a lawyer, a loveseat or even a lizard? The Yellow Pages has always been the place to turn and that still holds true on-line.*

▸ Search for a business by category or name.

▸ International business directories are also available.

▸ Print out coupons for extra savings.

Sites To Help You Simplify Your Life

# Additional Service Sites

Check out these other great sites! They're guaranteed to make your life just a little easier.

**1800flowers**.com – *flowers for every reason and season*

**555-1212**.com – *directory of individuals and businesses*

**abcnews.go**.com – *today's headlines, webcasts and more*

**cnn**.com – *national and world news at your fingertips*

**dataferret**.com – *record dates, phone numbers and more*

**dialpad**.com – *make phone calls through your computer*

**ftd**.com – *send flowers without having to leave your home*

**hotmail**.com – *sign up for a free e-mail account today*

**intellicast**.com – *weather forecasts for around the nation*

**iping**.com – *free service for wake-up and reminder calls*

**irs**.gov – *e-file your tax returns from home*

**mapquest**.com – *plan a road trip with their maps and guides*

**myhelpdesk**.com – *solutions to all of your computer problems*

**net2phone**.com – *get up to 60 minutes of free long distance*

**netradio**.com – *listen to the radio while you browse the web*

**page-a-day**.com – *download a calendar for your desktop*

**photoworks**.com – *post photos on-line for friends and family*

**prescriptionsbymail**.com – *free shipping for prescriptions*

**protonic**.com – *on-line community that provides tech support*

**remindall**.com – *service will e-mail you reminders of events*

**snapfish**.com – *get your film developed and posted on-line*

**weather**.com – *the official site of The Weather Channel*

**worldtimeserver**.com – *find out what time it is anywhere*

**zdnet**.com – *computer news, updates and troubleshooting*

# More Of The Best Websites

And then there's the rest of it: the websites that don't fit into any one specific category, but which are so useful/fun/clever that they just have to be mentioned. How could we not tell you, for instance, about the neat ways to get free stuff (and who out there doesn't love free stuff) like product samples and trial offers? Or the sites that let you sign up for contests and play games?

And there's so much more available on the Internet. We've shown you all the practical stuff on the 'net, but now see the fun stuff like joke and humor pages, multi-media portals and sites whose only reason for existence is to keep you entertained.

But that's STILL not all. In fact, the options are endless. Find what your future has to hold when you sneak a peak at your horoscope. There are even ways to relieve stress – whether its through sites that supply you with a variety of beautiful scenes of babbling brooks and green fields that you can turn into a screensaver or sites that feature downloads that let you take out your frustrations on an animated caricature of your boss! And it never hurts to know a good joke when you're trying to impress someone new!

Or you can send your friends a free e-greeting. For birthdays, holidays, or "just because," there are thousands of greetings that you can blast all over cyberspace with just a click of a mouse.

# 123greetings.com

*This site advertises "free greetings for the planet."*

▶ Find out about obscure holidays that you can send cards for. Did you know there's a "Hot Dog Day?"

▶ Get their free newsletter.

▶ Choose cards from their top-ranked greetings or hunt for one of your own.

# adcritic.com

*Some commercials are so entertaining that we need to see them again, while others never air for various reasons. This site lets you see both of these types of ads and more!*

▶ See never before-released commercials or view commercials from around the world.

▶ Rate commercials and voice your opinion.

▶ Get advertising industry news and shop the *adcritic.com* gear store.

# americangreetings.com

*One of the most popular e-card sites on-line, americangreetings.com has cards for every occasion – even those you may not have known existed.*

▶ Send e-cards or download and print paper cards to give in person.

▶ Play comics and games or send them as greetings.

▶ Send virtual kisses to friends and loved ones.

## amused.com

*You certainly will be amused when you click on this site. The ultimate waste of valuable time, surf their "Amusements" pages and columns for hours on end.*

- Great Shockwave games like "Stress Relief Aquarium," trivia games and personality tests.
- View categories like "New Stuff," "Amusements" and "Classics."
- Read columns and get links to other fab sites on the 'net.

## astrology.com

*Gaze into your future with the iVillage astrology page.*

- Get daily horoscopes and love scopes.
- Find out about your past lives and your karmic profile.
- Choose from more than 30 personalized profiles in the "ChartShop."

## atomicteen.com

*There's plenty to do and see on this e-zine devoted to entertaining teens of all ages on the 'net.*

- Get your horoscope, listen to music and do some shopping!
- There are sites for both "Boyz" and "Girlz."
- Find plenty of games, trivia and celebrity info to keep you busy.

More Of The Best Websites

## bluemountain.com

*A combination of terrific e-cards and multi-lingual translations (you can send your greetings in Japanese, Korean, Chinese, Italian, French, Spanish, or Portuguese) makes this one of the best cybergreeting sites around.*

- Monthly calendar suggests obscure special holidays such as "Blame Someone Else Day" and "No Housework Day."

- Video cards, party invitations, screensavers, voice greetings and gifts also available.

## classmates.com

*Fifteen million people have already signed up at classmates.com, hoping to find old school buddies. Free registration is the first step to re-connecting with your past.*

- 40,000 schools are listed throughout the U.S. and Canada.

- Space is devoted to class reunion updates.

- Message boards allow people to send widespread invitations.

- E-mail addresses are kept confidential.

## comics.com

*It doesn't have to be Sunday anymore to read the funny pages.*

- Never miss your favorite comic strips again!

- A new comic strip is featured daily.

- Editorial cartoons are also listed.

## egreetings.com

*Lots of these cards feature Flash animation and most have musical accompaniment.*

▸ Holiday calendar gives you excuses to send cards, such as "Kiss Your Mate Day" on April 28.

▸ Check back often for contests and incentives.

▸ "Music Scene" section features cards and music by popular stars such as Shaggy, Christina Aguilera and Barenaked Ladies.

▸ Gift certificates are available to send with your greetings.

## everythings-free.com

*Ah, the words we long to hear, "Everything's free." Too good to be true? Not on this site.*

▸ Freebies from all over the Internet are packaged in one handy site.

▸ Get everything from phone cards to CDs to cameras.

▸ Find stuff by category or browse from lists.

## flingthecow.com

*Cows are everywhere these days. They're even on the Internet, sitting atop a catapult, waiting for you to do some target practice.*

▸ Fling a cow across an open meadow onto a target for stress relief or silliness.

▸ The site will keep score and enter you into their "Hall of Fame" if you're good enough.

**More Of The Best Websites**

# joecartoon.com

*Joe Cartoon may be a bit crass now and then, but the site is a lot of fun and a great source of random, quirky, silly stuff.*

- Joe Cartoon is the official home of the "Frog in a Blender."
- Download cartoons or send them as greeting cards to friends.
- View animated cartoons.
- Sign up for the newsletter to be informed of new site additions.

# totallyfreestuff.com

*No strings attached, the stuff on this site is totally free.*

- Find and download free software and screensavers.
- Look for free jewelry, as well as health and body supplies.
- Find out how to get free cash just for surfing the 'net.

# utterlyfree.com

*Devoted to the art of getting something for nothing, this freebie site – updated daily – is your link to free product samples, on-line contests and more.*

- Loads of freebie categories include books, travel, phone stuff and miscellaneous.
- Join the free mailing list to be notified of new offers as they come in.
- Check out the "Top 15" freebies of the day.

# More Of
# "More Of The Best Websites"

Still have time on your hands? These sites should provide some more, uhm, enhancing, entertainment.

**atomfilms**.com - *watch independent movies in all genres*

**bored**.com - *a great portal site if you're looking to kill time*

**cinemanow**.com - *browse and watch films at home*

**comedyzone.beeb**.com - *read great humor articles*

**download**.com - *find software programs and games on-line*

**flipside**.com - *play games and win prizes in "Virtual Vegas"*

**free-daily-horoscopes**.com - *what does your future hold?*

**gamehouse**.com - *play casino, sport, action or board games*

**hampsterdance2**.com - *the lively hampsters are still at it*

**hotornot**.com - *rate endless pictures of men and women*

**humor**.com - *find comedians, diversions or chat with friends*

**ifilm**.com - *movie reviews and short films on the Internet*

**iwin**.com - *play games and tournaments to win prizes*

**joke-of-the-day**.com - *new laughs mailed to you every day*

**kissthisguy**.com - *a database of misheard song lyrics*

**muppetworld**.com - *humor from old friends, The Muppets*

**newsoftheweird**.com - *national or regional wacky news*

**quizland**.com - *trivia quizzes, crossworld puzzles and games*

**screensaver**.com - *spice up desktops with cool screensavers*

**theopinion**.com - *read opinions and voice any of yours*

**thespark**.com/paper_writer - *get (funny) lit or history papers*

**wackytimes**.com - *entertaining parody and "wacky" news*

**witcity**.com - *visit the funniest "town" on the Internet*

# Your Favorite Websites

Know of a good website that we didn't list? Record all of your on-line favorites on this page for easy access.

# E-mail Addresses

Keep all of your friends' and family's e-mail addresses here so that they are right at your fingertips whenever you need them!

| Name | E-mail Adddress |
|------|-----------------|
|      |                 |

# All The Best Websites™

## Check Out The Latest Titles In This Series!

### Packed With Reviews And Photos Of Hundreds Of The Greatest Websites!

### Look For These Titles And More At A Store Near You!

Each book contains 96 full-color pages and includes informative sections to help you *navigate the web* and *use the Internet to simplify your life!*

306 Industrial Park Road   Middletown, CT 06457   800-746-3686   CheckerBee.com